TRAE YOUNG

NBA STAR

By Douglas Lynne

Book design by Jake Slavik
Cover design by Jake Nordby

Photographs ©: Nick Wass/AP Images, cover, 1, 23; John Amis/AP Images, 4, 7, 8; Brian Rothmuller/Icon Sportswire/AP Images, 10; Steve Sisney/The Oklahoman/AP Images, 13; Matthew Visinsky/Icon Sportswire/AP Images, 14; Kevin Hagen/AP Images, 16; Austin McAfee/Icon Sportswire/AP Images, 19; David Banks/AP Images, 20; Red Line Editorial, 22

Press Box Books, an imprint of Press Room Editions.

Library of Congress Control Number: 2020901613

ISBN
978-1-63494-224-9 (library bound)
978-1-63494-242-3 (paperback)
978-1-63494-260-7 (epub)
978-1-63494-278-2 (hosted ebook)

Distributed by North Star Editions, Inc.
2297 Waters Drive
Mendota Heights, MN 55120
www.northstareditions.com

Printed in the United States of America
082020

ABOUT THE AUTHOR

Douglas Lynne is a freelance writer. He spent many years working in the media, first in newspapers and later for online organizations, covering everything from breaking news to politics to entertainment to sports. He lives in Minneapolis, Minnesota.

TABLE OF CONTENTS

ATLANTA
11
HAWKS

1

TAKING OVER

Trae Young was already having a good game against the Chicago Bulls on March 1, 2019. The National Basketball Association (NBA) rookie had 16 points through the first three quarters. Young then made a good night great. He scored 18 more points in the fourth quarter.

With 3:19 to go, Young stole the ball. He dribbled fast up the court and laid it in. His Atlanta Hawks scored nine more

Trae Young makes a pass to an open teammate during his big game against the Bulls.

points in a row. Young scored five of them. His layup gave them a 121–116 lead with one minute to go.

Chicago tied the game at 121–121. The Hawks had a chance to win it at the end. Young was the man to take the shot. The clock was ticking down under 10 seconds. Young dribbled closer to the three-point line. He took a step back and released a quick shot. It hit nothing but net.

Just 2.2 seconds remained on the clock. But Atlanta committed a foul and the Bulls were able to tie the game. It went into overtime. Young kept the Hawks in it. He made a layup with one second left to force a second overtime.

Young also focused on his defense against Chicago.

The Bulls got physical with Young, but he still kept scoring.

The Hawks kept battling. Young gave them a lead early in the second overtime. But they couldn't hold it. The game went to a third overtime. Then a fourth. Finally, the Hawks ran out of gas. They lost 168–161.

Young was upset about the loss. But he was proud of how his teammates kept fighting. Young finished with 49 points and 16 assists. He became the first rookie with 45 points and 10 assists in a game since Michael Jordan 34 years earlier. It was just another sign of the star he was becoming.

AMAZING RUN

The Bulls game was Young's third straight high-scoring game. He became the first player in 22 years to score 120 points over three games.

15
ALL-AMERICAN
CAMP

2

SUPER SOONER

Trae Young was born on September 19, 1998, in Lubbock, Texas. That's where his dad, Rayford Young, was playing basketball for Texas Tech.

The family moved to Norman, Oklahoma, to be closer to their relatives. But Rayford knew there was better basketball in Texas. He would make a three-hour drive to Dallas or a six-hour drive to Houston to take Trae to games.

Trae participates in a basketball camp in California before his senior year of high school.

The family also had season tickets to Oklahoma City Thunder games. Trae and his dad liked to arrive early for games. Trae watched how the pros warmed up and what they did to improve their skills.

TEAM USA

Trae got his first international experience after graduating from high school. He played on the USA Under-18 National Team in July 2016. The team went 5–0 and won the gold medal at the FIBA Americas U18 Championship.

It was clear in high school Trae would be a special basketball player. As a senior, he averaged more than 42 points per game. People came out just to see him play. Everyone wanted to know where he was going to college. He had to stop going to Thunder games because of the attention he drew.

Trae had the best colleges in the country after him. But in the end, he went with where he

Trae made a lot of people in Norman happy when he decided to go to the University of Oklahoma.

was most comfortable. He stayed home to play with the Oklahoma Sooners.

Trae scored in double figures in every game he played for the Sooners.

Trae's great scoring ability carried over to college. Early in the season, Oklahoma played in a tournament. Trae scored 28 points against Arkansas in the opening game. The next day he scored 33 against Portland. Two days later he poured in 43 against Oregon. Trae could score from anywhere.

But he also was great at running the offense. In December, Trae had 22 assists against Northwestern State. That tied the all-time college record. Trae led the country in both points and assists that year. After Oklahoma lost in the NCAA Tournament, he decided to enter the 2018 NBA Draft.

2017–18 NCAA DIVISION I
HIGHEST POINTS-PER-GAME AVERAGE

- **Trae Young**, Oklahoma, **27.4**
- **Kendrick Nunn**, Oakland, **25.9**
- **Jordan Howard**, Central Arkansas, **25.1**
- **Chris Clemons**, Campbell, **24.9**

THEY
will
KNOW
YOUR
NAME

3

LIKE A HAWK

Trae Young played just one college season. But it was an impressive one. It was so impressive NBA stars such as Stephen Curry and LeBron James said they'd been watching him play.

The Dallas Mavericks chose Young with the fifth pick in the 2018 NBA Draft. But they didn't keep him. They traded him to the Hawks for guard Luka Dončić and a future draft pick. The Hawks had picked

Young was drafted by the Dallas Mavericks but immediately traded to the Atlanta Hawks.

Dončić with the third pick. Some observers thought the Hawks would regret the trade.

Young did not perform well in summer league games. Then he made just five of 14 shots in his NBA debut. But he was the same scorer he'd always been. Young exploded for 35 points in his third game. He also dished out 11 assists. He was the second-youngest rookie to hit those totals in a game. The only one younger was LeBron James.

Young got better as the season went on. He and Dončić were the top candidates to be named NBA Rookie of the Year. Dončić ended up winning. But Young showed the trade was no mistake.

Young and Luka Dončić, *left*, battled it out for the NBA Rookie of the Year Award.

Young celebrates after making a three-pointer during his first NBA All-Star Game in 2020.

Heading into his second season, the question was whether Young could improve on his impressive rookie year. He gave a quick answer by scoring 38 points in the 2019–20 season opener.

Young was scoring like an All-Star. He drew comparisons to Curry. Despite Atlanta's poor record, Young was considered one of the best guards in the league. He was selected to his first NBA All-Star Game in February 2020.

TRIBUTE TO KOBE

Kobe Bryant was a mentor to Young. When Bryant died in January 2020, Young wanted to honor him. He wore jersey No. 8 that Bryant wore for the first eight seconds of a game. Then he changed back to his normal No. 11. Young went on to score 45 points that night.

Making the All-Star Game was a dream come true. But Young was only 21. He had plenty more dreams to accomplish.

TIMELINE MAP

1. **Lubbock, Texas: 1998**
   Trae Young is born on September 19.
2. **Norman, Oklahoma: 2017**
   Young graduates from Norman North High School.
3. **Norman, Oklahoma: 2017**
   On December 22, Young ties the college record with 22 assists in a game for the Oklahoma Sooners.
4. **Brooklyn, New York: 2018**
   Young is drafted fifth by the Dallas Mavericks, then traded to the Atlanta Hawks for Luka Dončić on June 21.
5. **New York, New York: 2018**
   Young makes his NBA debut on October 17, scoring 14 points in a loss to the New York Knicks.
6. **Atlanta, Georgia: 2019**
   Young scores a career-high 49 points in a four-overtime loss to the Chicago Bulls on March 1.
7. **Indianapolis, Indiana: 2019**
   On November 29, Young ties a career high with 49 points in a loss to the Indiana Pacers.
8. **Chicago, Illinois: 2020**
   Young starts and plays in his first NBA All-Star Game on February 16, leading his team with 10 assists.

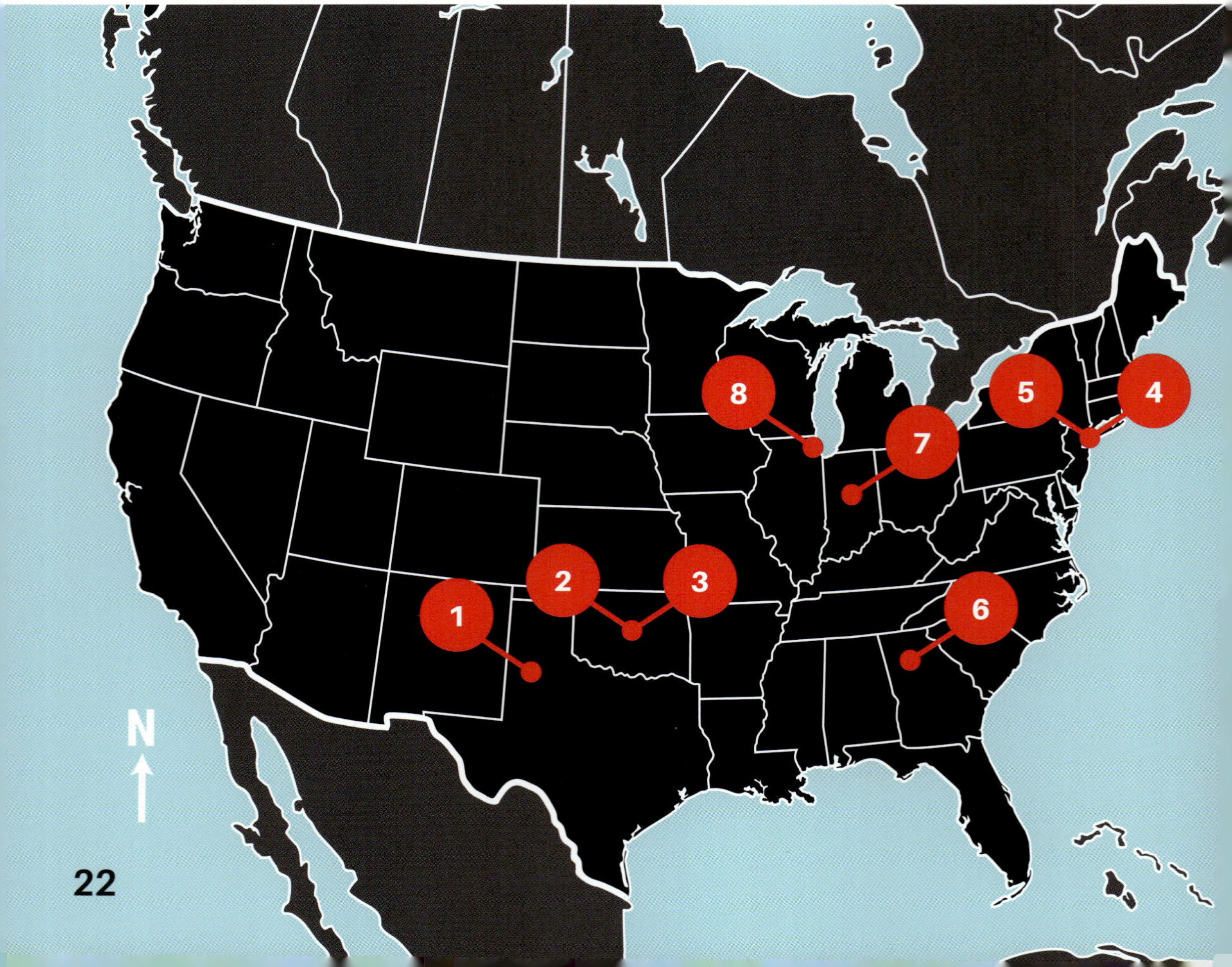

AT-A-GLANCE

TRAE YOUNG

Birth date: September 19, 1998

Birthplace: Lubbock, Texas

Position: Point guard

Height: 6 feet 1 inch

Weight: 180 pounds

Current team: Atlanta Hawks (2018–)

Past team: Oklahoma Sooners (2017–18)

Major awards: NBA All-Star (2020), NBA All-Rookie First Team (2019), Wayman Tisdale Award for National Freshman Player of the Year (2018)

Accurate through the 2019–20 season.

MORE INFORMATION

To learn more about Trae Young, go to **pressboxbooks.com/AllAccess**.

These links are routinely monitored and updated to provide the most current information available.

GLOSSARY

assist

A pass that leads to a made shot in basketball.

draft

A system by which sports leagues divide up new talent.

foul

A violation of the rules that involve physical contact with an opponent.

layup

A shot taken near the basket, often by bouncing the ball off the backboard.

mentor

A person who gives advice and guidance to another person.

rookie

A first-year player.

INDEX

The Engine

The Hellcat has an amazing sound. Its roar comes from a 6.2-liter HEMI V-8 engine. It's supercharged. Superchargers push more air into engines. More air means more power. The car's top speed is 199 miles (320 kilometers) per hour.

Spinning Tires

Drivers can set the cars' traction. Traction is how well the tires grip the road. With less traction, cars can **drift**. The back wheels can spin. They squeal and smoke.

Dodge built the engine in secret. The company didn't want anyone to know how powerful it would be.

By the Numbers

about **22** miles (35 km) per gallon

ESTIMATED HIGHWAY **MILEAGE**

5

TOTAL SEATING

75.7 INCHES (192 CM) **WIDTH** WITHOUT MIRRORS

197.5
INCHES
(502 CM)
LENGTH

3.6
SECONDS

TIME TO GO FROM
0 to 60 MILES
(97 KM) PER HOUR
WITH AUTOMATIC TRANSMISSION

ABOUT
$65,495
BASE PRICE

In 2018, Dodge revealed the 2019 Hellcat and Hellcat Redeye. The new Hellcat has 717 horsepower. The Redeye has a massive 797 horsepower.

CHAPTER 4

An Epic Car

The Hellcat is a fan favorite. Its power will thrill drivers for years to come. People expect its classic style will stay the same. But Dodge is known for keeping secrets. Car lovers will just have to wait and see.

caliper (KAL-uh-per)—a device used to press a brake pad against the sides of a brake rotor

drift (DRIFT)—to break traction with the back of the car and slide through a curve

fender (FEN-der)—the part of a car's side that goes around a wheel

horsepower (HORS-pow-uhr)—a unit used to measure the power of engines

hulking (HUHL-king)—very large or heavy

mileage (MAHY-lij)—the average number of miles a vehicle will travel on a gallon of gasoline

muscle car (MUHS-uhl KAHR)—an American-made car with a powerful engine designed for straight-line driving

spoiler (SPOI-ler)—a device placed on a vehicle to reduce lift and increase drag; it "spoils" the airflow.

transmission (trans-MISH-uhn)—a group of parts that takes energy from the engine to an axle that moves

valet (va-LEY)—a person who parks cars for guests at a hotel or restaurant

BOOKS

Fishman, Jon M. *Cool Muscle Cars*. Awesome Rides. Minneapolis: Lerner Publications, 2019.

Oachs, Emily Rose. *Dodge Challenger SRT Hellcat*. Car Crazy. Minneapolis: Bellwether Media, Inc., 2017.

Westcott, Jim. *Performance Cars*. Rank It! Mankato, MN: Black Rabbit Books, 2018.

WEBSITES

2018 Dodge Challenger
www.dodge.com/challenger.html

Dodge Challenger SRT Hellcat Widebody
www.edmunds.com/dodge/challenger/2018/srt-hellcat-widebody/

Dodge Challenger SRT / SRT Hellcat
www.caranddriver.com/dodge/challenger-srt-srt-hellcat

INDEX